PRIMARY READERS
PRE-STARTERS

Callum the Caterpillar

Jane Cadwallader
Illustrator: Fhiona Galloway

Callum the Caterpillar is sad.

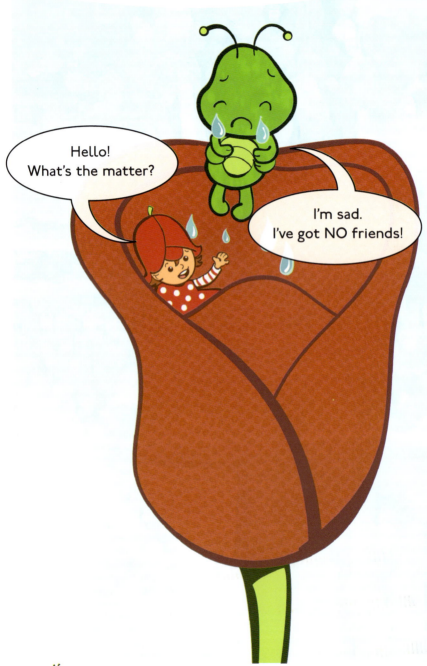

Look at the caterpillar

Big caterpillars, little caterpillars, long caterpillars,

here are caterpillars everywhere!

short caterpillars, fat caterpillars
and thin caterpillars.

Callum is in the park. Look at the caterpillars!

There are caterpillars
everywhere!

Oh no!
There is no space for me!

Oh dear!

Callum is in the kitchen. Look at the caterpillars!

There are caterpillars everywhere!
Under the chairs and in the fridge
and on the table!

Callum goes to the bedroom.
Callum is sleepy. Cathy is sleepy too.

Oh no! There are caterpillars everywhere!
On the bed and under the table and in the wardrobe!

Callum goes to see the little red fairy. He is not happy!

Callum is tired. He goes to bed.

Look! Look at the butterflies!

There is a red and yellow butterfly, and a blue and green butterfly.

There's a black and white butterfly and a purple and brown butterfly.

There is a grey and orange butterfly and a yellow and pink butterfly.

Now there is space for Callum and **all** his friends.

Picture Dictionary